FEMALE FIGURE SKATING LEGENDS

Oksana Baiul

Nicole Bobek

Ekaterina Gordeeva

Nancy Kerrigan

Michelle Kwan

Tara Lipinski

Katarina Witt

Kristi Yamaguchi

CHELSEA HOUSE PUBLISHERS

KRISTI
YAMAGUCHI

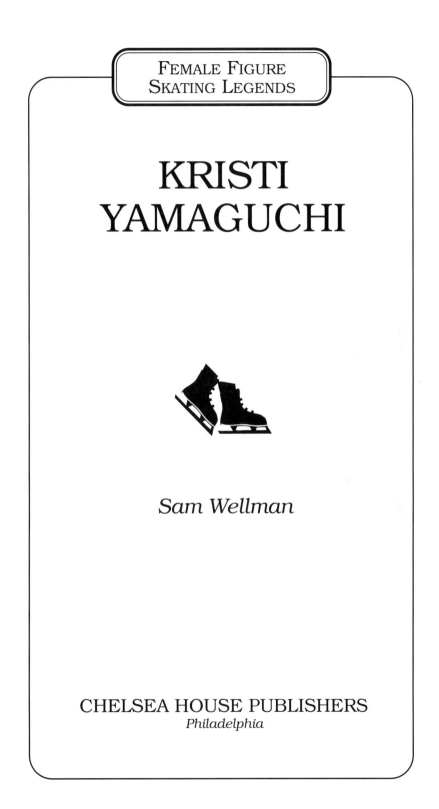

Sam Wellman

CHELSEA HOUSE PUBLISHERS
Philadelphia

Produced by Choptank Syndicate, Inc.

Editor and Picture Researcher: Norman L. Macht
Production Coordinator and Editorial Assistant: Mary E. Hull
Design and Production: Lisa Hochstein

CHELSEA HOUSE PUBLISHERS

Editor in Chief: Stephen Reginald
Managing Editor: James Gallagher
Production Manager: Pamela Loos
Art Director: Sara Davis
Director of Photography: Judy L. Hasday
Senior Production Editor: Lisa Chippendale
Publishing Coordinator: James McAvoy
Cover Illustration: Keith Trego

Cover Photos: AP/Wide World Photos

The Chelsea House World Wide Web site address is
http://www.chelseahouse.com

3 5 7 9 8 6 4 2

Library of Congress Cataloging-in-Publication Data

Wellman, Sam.
    Kristi Yamaguchi / Sam Wellman.
      p.   cm. — (Female figure skating legends)
    Includes bibliographical references (p.   ) and index.
    Summary: A biography of the young Japanese American figure
  skater who won a gold medal at the 1992 Olympics and has since
  become a professional figure skater.
    ISBN 0-7910-5025-4 (hc)
    1. Yamaguchi, Kristi—Juvenile literature. 2. Skaters—
  United States—Biography—Juvenile literature. [1. Yamaguchi, Kristi.
  2. Ice skaters. 3. Women—Biography. 4. Japanese Americans—Biography.]
  I. Title. II. Series.
  GV850.Y36W45 1998
  796.91'2'092—dc21   98-21903
  [b]   CIP
                                                               AC

CONTENTS

OLYMPIC GOLD

The date was February 21, 1992. Thousands of people packed the ice-skating arena in Albertville, France at the 1992 winter Olympics. Waiting to skate was a tiny American, the reigning world and U.S. champion, Kristi Yamaguchi. A few days earlier Kristi had skated her short program to Strauss's "Blue Danube" waltz, and she was in the lead for the gold as she waited for her turn to perform the long program. As she waited, Kristi was shocked when a woman walked up to her and hugged her and wished her luck.

She recognized her well-wisher as her life-long idol Dorothy Hamill, the 1976 Olympic figure-skating champion. Hamill was the last American woman to win the gold medal. Many Americans, including a young

Kristi Yamaguchi, dressed in blue and teal, performs her short program to "The Blue Danube" at the 1992 Olympics.

Kristi Yamaguchi, had watched on television as Hamill won the gold. Dorothy Hamill became so popular after the 1976 Olympics, she inspired a new hair style as thousands of American women chose to cut their hair like hers. A toy manufacturer even designed a Dorothy Hamill doll, and Kristi had begged her parents for one. Dorothy Hamill was Kristi's childhood idol, and now, at one of the most crucial moments in Kristi's life, Dorothy had come up to her and hugged her!

A thousand thoughts swirled around Kristi as she prepared for her long program. In 1976 Dorothy Hamill had eight double jumps in her long program—jumps where she would launch herself and spin two revolutions before landing cleanly on one skate blade. In contrast, Kristi was expected to do much more than that. She had to spin around three times to do triple jumps. Her legs seemed too thin and her feet too small to perform the seven triples scheduled for her long program. Increasingly, skaters were incorporating more and more complicated jumps into their programs in order to win high marks. Skating was moving away from an emphasis on artistic moves and grace; now it meant jumping higher than ever before and with tremendous strength. Recently, a female skater, Tonya Harding, had hit one of the first triple Axels ever landed in a ladies' competition. Kristi had tried and tried, but she had yet to master the triple Axel.

Kristi's main rival in the competition, Midori Ito of Japan, was also doing the triple Axel, and was one of a select few female skaters who had ever landed it. Yet those who were able to do the triple Axel had raised the bar in competition, making it harder for those who could not master the jump to remain competitive.

Midori Ito of Japan was Kristi's main rival in the 1992 Olympics. Ito had mastered the triple Axel, the one jump that Kristi could not do.

How many times had reporters asked Kristi, "Don't you need the triple Axel jump to win?" In fact, it was just three months ago—on this very ice in France—that Midori Ito had landed the triple Axel and beaten Kristi in the Trophy Lalique. Kristi had to admit it was spectacular the way Ito would dash across the ice and launch herself off the outside edge of her left skate blade. Ito seemed in orbit as she spun three and one half revolutions before landing on her right skate blade.

The press was billing the showdown between Yamaguchi and Ito as a battle between artistry and athleticism, but Kristi maintained that she had combined both elements into her program. "A lot of people look at me as a skater with an artistic side, but I still have seven triples planned in my program," Kristi had responded defensively to one reporter.

Her coach, Christy Ness, had defended her too. She insisted to a *Sporting News* reporter that Kristi's opening combination of a triple Lutz jump followed immediately by a triple toe loop jump was the equal of a triple Axel in terms of difficulty. Coach Ness told the same reporter that "All this indiscriminate jumping kind of puts me off. I see a lot of misses on jumps in competition, and a clean program will beat that nearly every time." And yet, in another interview Coach Ness had been cold comfort to Kristi as she admitted that without the triple Axel jump, ". . . you have one less trick in your bag." Without that jump, it would be difficult to win the gold.

Kristi also had to do one kind of jump—the triple Salchow—that gave her fits. For the Salchow, Kristi had to skate backwards, then jump up from a back inside skate edge, revolve three times, and land on the outside edge of her opposite skate. She once hadn't been able to land it cleanly for a whole year. But that was ancient history, Kristi reminded herself. Veteran skaters warned Kristi of that "nasty little voice" that chattered doubts in a skater's mind just before a performance. But Kristi's Olympic roommate Nancy Kerrigan was the worrier, not Kristi.

Kristi forced herself to block out all distractions. She flounced the gold ribbon that tied her long ponytail. She checked her special earrings; the right pearl was plain, but the left pearl dangled a heart for courage. She reminded herself that no one designed nicer costumes than Lauren Sheehan, who designed her long-sleeved

black and gold costume. She reminded herself
no one styled nicer skating routines than Sandra
Bezic, who styled her long program. In her mind
now she ran through her program, imagining
herself performing every element to perfection.
"Okay, get out there, skate, like it's an everyday
practice," Kristi snapped at herself sternly.

"Kristi Yamaguchi," boomed the arena's
sound system.

Kristi's cousin hugs
her and other family
members greet her as
she arrives back home
in California following
her Olympic victory at
the 1992 Olympics in
Albertville, France.

Suddenly she was gliding toward center ice. She clasped her hands behind her back and posed for the start. Focus, focus, focus. She blocked out all thoughts but her program. No parents, no sister Lori, no brother Brett. She blocked out all sights. No television cameras. No eager faces. Kristi also blocked out the excited murmuring from the audience. The only sound she would respond to now was the stirring music of "Malagueña." The Spanish rhythm began. Automatic from hundreds of repetitions, Kristi glided gracefully toward the most difficult element of her routine, her combination triple Lutz–triple toe loop jump. Up. Around three times. Up. Around three times. She landed the back-to-back jumps cleanly. Then she completed a triple flip jump. Clean. Just like practice— relax, relax, relax. She entered the slower tempo of her music and launched her triple loop jump. She landed awkwardly and had to touch the ice with one hand to keep from falling.

The crowd groaned.

She had been too relaxed, and did not fight to save the jump. Although she wanted to jump out of her skin because of the near fall, she had to remain focused. Coming up in nine seconds was the jump that gave her fits, the triple Salchow. She had only seconds to decide if she should cut it to a double jump. Changing a program that she had practiced hundreds of times was very dangerous. It could destroy her pace. All her years of skating experience came to bear; in a flash she changed the triple Salchow to a double and landed it easily. The tempo of her music got faster. Focused, she exploded to land a triple Lutz, the jump second only to the triple Axel in difficulty. Finally, she landed her last jump, a double Axel, and finished in a dazzling straight-up spin.

The crowd deafened her with applause. Flowers rained onto the ice. Kristi seemed under an avalanche of love. She waved and smiled, choking back tears, then glided to the waiting area skaters called the "kiss and cry" box. *New York Times* reporter Michael Janofsky would later describe her performance, writing: "Yamaguchi crafted. . . a feathery vision of artistic precision and elegance, with near total disdain for the latest trends in acrobatic jumping." She had performed, he said, "as if all that mattered was making people smile."

Kristi had been skating seriously for 12 years. She knew she had left the door wide open for her competitors to beat her. She had cleanly landed only five triple jumps. There would be no perfect 6.0s given for her performance this day, the most important day of her life. She could be beaten by another skater's flawless performance.

Though she had won the short program a few days earlier with high marks from all nine of the judges, Kristi could still lose her chance at the gold medal if another skater outperformed her in the long program. With her coach beside her, Kristi listened tensely for her scores. First came the technical scores. Four of the nine judges gave her 5.8s; five gave her 5.7s. If her artistic scores were also low she would surely be bested by both Nancy Kerrigan and Midori Ito. Then came the scores for artistry: one 5.8 and eight 5.9s.

Kristi felt sick. The long program counted twice as much as the short program in a skater's final score. If Nancy Kerrigan, in second place after the short program, surpassed Kristi in the long Nancy would win the gold medal.

"Nancy Kerrigan," boomed the sound system.

Nancy was an artistic skater like Kristi. She

Kristi Yamaguchi stands with silver medalist Midori Ito and bronze medalist Nancy Kerrigan during the ceremonies at the 1992 Olympics.

flowed from element to element seamlessly. But Kristi could see that Nancy was rattled, almost gasping for air. Nancy missed her combination triple-double jump, and cut two triple jumps back to singles, but she did not fall. Her scores were respectable but no match for Kristi's.

France's Surya Bonaly was in third place after the short program. A powerful jumper like Midori Ito, she planned an unheard-of eight triple jumps and one quadruple jump. She would certainly win gold with a perfect skate of such a difficult program. But Bonaly proved tighter than Nancy Kerrigan, missing three triples and mangling the quadruple. Kristi was happy for Nancy, who was now certain to win a medal. As Kristi waited to hear Bonaly's scores she saw the big blue eyes of Coach Ness grow even wider. Suddenly Kristi realized this was her moment of certainty too. If Bonaly's scores in the long program were lower than Kristi's, then in the complex scoring system of figure skating Kristi had won the gold medal—no matter how well Midori Ito skated when it was her turn.

Kristi could scarcely breathe. Her lifelong dream was within reach. When Bonaly's scores boomed across the arena like cannon shots, Kristi Yamaguchi was the Olympic champion.

BORN IMPAIRED

No one who saw Kristi Tsuya Yamaguchi when she was born on July 12, 1971, in Hayward, California, would ever have expected her to become a world-class athlete. It wasn't because the baby of Jim and Carole Yamaguchi was tiny, although she weighed less than six pounds. Baby Kristi's feet curled inward, seeming as useless as dead leaves.

Her father was a dentist and her mother a medical secretary, so they knew deformed feet at birth were probably not permanent. Nevertheless it was almost heartbreaking to see the tiny two-week-old infant with casts on her feet. After the casts came off Kristi had to keep her feet straight for a very long time while the bones aligned themselves correctly as they grew. Forced to wear braces at all times, even

Kristi begged her parents for skating lessons after she saw Dorothy Hamill perform at the 1976 Olympics.

17

Members of the New York City Ballet perform the Nutcracker. *Kristi, who took ballet lessons when she was only four years old, loved the fancy costumes ballerinas got to wear and enjoyed dressing up for ballet recitals.*

when she slept, she had few moments without pain. When she was about one year old she wore corrective shoes and put on the braces at night.

Her feet turned in more than normal, but gradually only the worried eyes of her parents noticed. Otherwise, Kristi bustled through the usual activities of a toddler, then a pre-schooler. The Yamaguchis lived in Hayward, and a few years later in Fremont, both cities of about 100,000 on the east side of San Francisco Bay. Few weather hazards there slowed a child. In a climate that was rarely above 70 degrees or below 40 degrees, with little wind or rain, a child could go full speed indoors or outdoors.

Kristi had plenty of action at home. She played and squabbled with sister Lori, who was two years older. When Kristi was three along came a baby brother, Brett. At four Kristi took ballet lessons. She loved the recital. In addition to dainty ballet slippers she got to wear a fluffy costume and a fancy ribbon in her hair. She even got to flaunt a wand with a star on top. But at the age of five she discovered the ultimate in fancy costume displays. An ice skating rink at the mall held an ice show. Not only were the girls splendid in colorful costumes, but they glided, almost floated across the ice. "Kristi fell in love with it," observed her mother.

After that display Kristi never stopped asking for ice skating lessons. About the same time, Kristi saw on television a beautiful woman named Dorothy Hamill win a gold medal in figure skating at the 1976 winter Olympics. Getting a Dorothy Hamill doll was almost as good as getting skating lessons—but not quite. She kept asking for lessons. Her mother insisted that she had to learn to read first. Kristi tackled reading furiously.

When she was six her mother took her for her first lessons at the mall. As an instructor put the huge skates on her feet Kristi dreamed that one day she would do what Dorothy Hamill did. Soon Kristi let go of the wooden barrier around the rink and joined a group of wobbly wide-eyed children out on the ice. Once they were stable enough to avoid falling down every few seconds their instructor taught them to "scull" or "swizzle." With their heels together and toes out, they bent their knees, and coasted slowly across the ice. Then they turned their toes in and slowly stopped. After a while they were sculling around the ice in large circles. Then they learned to do the same thing backwards. Some of the students, including Kristi, fell again and again. They were taught to relax,

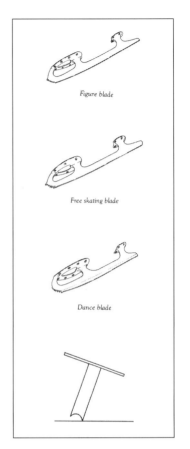

Figure blade

Free skating blade

Dance blade

There are several types of skate blades. The figure at the bottom shows the inside and outside edges of a skate blade as well as the groove between them. A skater uses the different blade edges to perform.

Kristi's skates provided ankle support, but they looked nothing like this ladies' skate, which dates from the 1860s.

to crumple like rag dolls. Kristi didn't mind. She felt like she was imitating her Dorothy Hamill doll. Sometimes she carried the doll with her.

Falling while relaxed was rarely painful. Soon the children learned to skate forward and backward without sculling. Arch your back, but not too much, urged the instructor. Palms down. Hold your hands like graceful flowers, girls. Elbows in. The children learned to skate forward and backward on one foot, turning by switching feet in a "crossover." Kristi would remember later hearing her mother say how very weak she was the first few times she put on skates. Her mother's voice choked up as she described how Kristi couldn't do simple back crossovers. She struggled so hard her tiny body was all hunched over. Still Kristi refused to quit. When she got herself gliding across the ice she felt a freedom and a joy she had never known before.

"When I'm skating I feel like I can do anything; I feel like I can stay out there forever," she explained years later.

Kristi soon had her own skates. Each skate blade was grooved with an outside edge and an inside edge. At the front of each blade were saw-teeth called the toe pick. For certain elements the instructor might specify "forward outside," "forward inside," "back outside," "back inside" or even "toe." These were the blade positions. The blades were rigidly attached to skate boots of stiff leather with rigid support around the ankles. Kristi also needed clothing appropriate for the ice. It was so cold skaters were always wiping their noses with tissue. From the beginning Kristi had to wear gloves while practicing. Although warmth was important, the clothing had to be loose enough to be comfortable.

The next step, according to the instructor, was to join an official skating club. That way Kristi could compete in official events of the United States Figure Skating Association (USFSA). Her mother was not sure Kristi should compete, but Kristi begged to be able to wear a nice rink costume. Although she didn't join an official skating club, she was allowed to compete in an event sponsored by the mall rink. Out of 13 competitors Kristi placed 12th. But she was having too much fun to quit.

Although she remained very small for her age, she seemed to get much stronger. She ate huge meals, always asking for spaghetti or cheese fondue. She was no longer at the bottom of the skating class. She began doing little jumps. The bunny hop came first—jumping off one skate and landing on the other. Then she advanced to the waltz jump. As she skated forward she jumped off one foot, turned one-half revolution in the air, and landed on the

Skating outdoors was not an option for Kristi Yamaguchi, who grew up in California. So Kristi's parents bought her ice time at an indoor rink where she could practice year-round.

other foot skating backwards. Kristi didn't fall down very often.

Although the Yamaguchis both had well-paying professions, they knew that serious skating was expensive. Besides paying for individual instruction, the skater also had to buy ice time to practice between lessons. The total cost could easily exceed $1000 for one year. But skating was like powerful therapy to the little girl.

The Yamaguchis took Kristi to 27-year-old coach Christy Kjarsgaard. She was startled to learn that tiny Kristi, who looked more Brett's age of five, was eight. But she studied Kristi intently. She told the parents matter-of-factly that Kristi would need to join the Palomares Figure Skating Club and skate in official USFSA competitions. Kristi would need many lessons. The compulsory figures for competition took hundreds of hours to learn. Kristi would need many hours of ice time. Her equipment would have to be better, even though she would quickly outgrow it. The expense would be even greater than Kristi's parents had guessed.

Her parents took a deep breath. Yes, they were willing.

3

HARD TRAINING

Serious skating requires a major commitment of time, determination, and money. Kristi's coach explained that this was no couple-of-hours twice-a-week endeavor. Kristi would have to practice three or four hours nonstop at least five or six days a week. Her parents looked at Kristi doubtfully. Kristi hugged her Dorothy Hamill doll and thought very hard about skating so many hours every day. To her it sounded more like fun than work.

If Coach Kjarsgaard had known Kristi had tried to bleach her long black hair so she could look like blond Farah Fawcett on the television show *Charlie's Angels*, she might have hesitated to take such a diminutive rebel as a student. Fortunately, Kristi's hair, which turned red rather than blond, grew fast. That stunt might

Kristi Yamaguchi carefully traces a compulsory figure while a judge watches. Kristi spent hours practicing school figures, which would count for a third of her overall score at competitions.

have been the last playful act of her life, because Kristi was now busy almost every hour of the day.

There was not enough time to get all the ice time she needed after school, so Kristi began to rise at four o'clock in the morning. After a bowl of cereal, her mother drove her to the rink where she practiced several hours before school. Then, as other children, still groggy from sleep, were starting school, Kristi would join them. And in the early evening when other children were still up watching television Kristi had to go to bed.

Like most young skaters, Kristi loved to jump up and spin in the air. Her coach taught her that all jumps were landed while skating backwards. But only the one called the Axel, the most difficult of jumps, was launched skating forward. She learned the subtle differences in the jumps. They were distinguished by the blade positions on the takeoff foot and the landing foot. For example, the simplest jump, the toe loop, was launched off the toepick of the free foot and landed on the back outside edge of the same foot. Kristi learned the order of increasing difficulty for the jumps: the toe loop, the Salchow, the loop, the flip, the Lutz, and the notorious Axel.

Through the years skaters kept perfecting more and more complicated jumps. The first triple jump in competition was completed by Dick Button in the 1952 winter Olympics. It was Button who said falling down is not the sign of a poor skater, but is the sign of a skater who never stops trying to improve. Kristi learned that the triple Axel was so difficult it had been completed for the first time only the previous year, in 1978 by Vern Taylor of Canada. No woman had ever done one. Nobody had ever

Harvard graduate Dick Button, shown here in a sit spin, was the first skater to complete a triple jump in competition when he landed a triple loop at the 1952 winter Olympics.

done a quadruple jump. Kristi would not be happy until she mastered every kind of jump.

Her coach emphasized the importance of learning body control. Ballet was the ultimate form of body control. So Kristi once again took ballet lessons. She learned the dancer's gestures for basic emotions: excitement, sadness, joy, love, fear, and bravado. These, she was told by her coach, were used in interpreting music on ice too.

Kristi also spent many hours on the ice learning the compulsory figures, or the school figures, as some called them. There were 42 figures, all based on different combinations of circles. Skaters had to retrace the figure with each skate. Judges would get down on their knees and squint at the ice to see how closely the skater's different traces lined up with each other. For a particular competition three of the 42 figures were chosen, their degree of difficulty matching the level of competition. The skater's skill in tracing the three figures accounted for 30 percent of their overall score. The compulsory figures once accounted for over half the skater's score, but over the years their relative importance in the final score was steadily whittled down.

Many in skating wanted to do away with the compulsories completely. They thought the appeal of skating to the general public was harmed by the compulsory figures. Competitions were often won by skaters who were masterful in the compulsories but were mediocre in the short and long programs of free skating. Because most spectators saw only the free skating on television they were baffled when the medals were awarded. "How could such a lackluster skater finish in first place?" wondered spectators. More and more skating officials, especially among the Americans, wanted to eliminate the compulsory figures from competition.

Canada's Vern Taylor became the first person to land a triple Axel when he successfully completed three and a half mid-air rotations during the 1978 Worlds in Ottawa.

The first time Kristi watched a more advanced skater trace the compulsory figure called the "serpentine" she hoped very much that compulsories would be done away with. The serpentine was supposed to look like three circles about 15 feet across and stacked on each other. Only two pushoffs were allowed during one complete serpentine. To make it even more of a nightmare, it had to be retraced, using the same skate blade positions, then it had to be retraced just as many times after switching blade positions and skating in the opposite directions.

Skaters dreaded compulsory figures. But a serious skater who wanted to compete had to learn them. Often now Kristi practiced without instruction. Her parents bought her ice time on the rink, where she had her own patch of ice, to practice her compulsory figures. But free skating had to be practiced just as rigorously as the compulsories. Occasionally a more advanced skater needed the whole rink because free skating required the use of the entire frozen surface. Skaters had to glide dangerously close to the boards during their dashes and jumps.

Kristi learned how artistry was defined in Rule 323 of The United States Figure Skating Association Rulebook:

In the marking of composition and style, the following must be considered:

(a) harmonious composition of
    the program as a whole and its
    conformity to the music chosen
(b) utilization of space
(c) easy movement and sureness
    in time to the music
(d) carriage
(e) originality
(f) expression of the character of music.

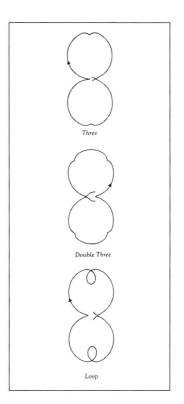

Three

Double Three

Loop

In the compulsory competitions, skaters are judged by the accuracy of the visible tracings their skates leave on the ice. Beginning from a stationary position, a skater may be asked to create any one of the dozens of different school figures, of which three are shown here. Each figure is made with either an inside or outside blade edge; the skater is never allowed to skate on the flat blade.

In the 1960s, the compulsory figures were an important aspect of competition. By the 1990s judges were rating skaters more on the artistic and technical aspects of their freeskating programs rather than the accuracy of their school figures.

Artistry was becoming more and more important in the judging of free skating. Yet the technical portion could not be ignored either. Coach Kjarsgaard told Kristi that for technical marks the judges weighed three factors: difficulty of the program, variety displayed, and the skill with which the elements were performed. It was obvious if Kristi was serious about competing she would have to master as great a variety of elements as she could, right up to the most difficult jumps. Not only jumps and spins and turns and steps had to be displayed, but they had to be done cleanly and all with apparent ease.

Kristi knew from watching great skaters compete on television that they usually scored from 5.5 to 5.9 out of a perfect 6.0. It was in that small range of scoring that the battles were fought among the very best skaters. That was the range that Kristi dreamed of attaining.

Then one day her coach stunned her by asking if she was ready for her first real USFSA competition.

4

TEENAGE SUCCESSES

Butterflies by the millions swirled inside Kristi. At the age of nine she skated in her first official competition—as a pre-juvenile, the lowest of the six levels of USFSA competition. Competition seemed scary at first, but she discovered that she adored everything about competing: the ice, the music, the judges, the bright costumes, and the excitement and encouragement of her coach and family. Kristi's grandparents especially enjoyed watching her perform. Though she was still very small for her age, Kristi finished fifth in her first official competition, a long way from the frail child who had to hunch over in her mighty effort to perform a crossover. On the ice she was strong. Her energy seemed unlimited. "I don't think she ever thinks of being tired," said her coach.

The USFSA skating competitions are divided into six levels: Kristi was nine when she began competing at the lowest level, the pre-juvenile.

An aspiring skater could compete at higher levels only by first passing a test given by three USFSA skating officials. Beyond Kristi's pre-juvenile level were juvenile, intermediate, novice, junior, and senior. The local competition was part of the Central Pacific Region. If she was good enough to finish in the top four in the Regional, she could advance to the Pacific Coast Sectional, which took the top four skaters from each of the three Regionals. The top four of those 12 went on to the National Championships, usually referred to as the Nationals.

Kristi could scarcely imagine competing at Nationals as a senior, the highest level. Besides the most difficult compulsory figures, a senior had to master the most forbidding elements for the free skate. Four different double jumps, including the Lutz, had to be performed. The senior had to execute two kinds of combination jumps with no steps in between. Four kinds of spins were mandatory, including one flying spin. And a very complicated serpentine step sequence had to be performed.

As a pre-juvenile Kristi could do none of that. Her most difficult elements were a single Lutz jump and a combination of two single jumps. Still, no one worked more tirelessly than Kristi. By the age of 11, Kristi made it to the 1982 Central Pacific Regional as a juvenile. There she met Coach Jim Hulick and 13-year-old skater Rudy Galindo. Galindo was looking for a partner to skate with him in pairs competition. He had a problem: he was only 4' 6" inches tall and bone thin. He had to lift his partner high in the air. Most girls his age were taller and heavier than he was. Then he and his coach met the tiny Kristi Yamaguchi.

Coach Hulick asked Kristi's parents if they would permit her to skate pairs with Rudy

under his tutelage. He and Rudy worked out of San Jose, just 15 miles south of Fremont. Kristi's parents wanted her to enjoy herself, and left it up to her. Kristi had seen Rudy skate, and the idea of working with another skater on the ice thrilled her. It seemed so grown up. But she wanted to continue her singles skating too. Coach Kjarsgaard was concerned about Kristi dividing her time between singles and pairs skating. They had worked together for six years. But she wanted Kristi to have fun. So Kristi began to train under two coaches and to practice two skating disciplines.

One element of pairs competition was the exciting overhead lift, where the boy lifted the girl high above his head. The lift was followed by the girl dropping back to the ice while twisting. Side-by-side in unison the partners had to do one jump, as well as one spin. Spinning together with one change of foot

Kristi began skating pairs with Rudy Galindo when she was 11. In 1986, the couple won the junior pairs competition at the Nationals in Long Island, New York.

At first Kristi feared the pairs throws, death spirals, and other risky moves associated with pairs skating, but as they practiced, she became more comfortable. Kristi appears to be flying over her partner Rudy Galindo's head in this maneuver, performed at the 1988 international free skating competition in Tokyo.

and one change of position intrigued Kristi. Many elements of pairs skating sounded easier than singles. However, she wasn't looking forward to the element called the "death spiral," where Rudy would hold her by one hand as she spun around him with her head just inches off the ice. When performed correctly, the death spiral made it appear that the man was pulling a woman up from the edge of a cliff; she would spiral down toward the ice and then the man would lift her up slowly until she was standing on her own once again.

In the next three years both young skaters picked up new skills and polished old skills. Kristi kept a steady gaze on her goals of reaching the Nationals and beyond. She asked her parents if she could drop out of school after completing the eighth grade and be privately tutored. They looked stunned, but they agreed. Skating had truly gained control over their lives. Kristi's costumes were sewn by a friend and Carole Yamaguchi beaded them. Choice skates now cost about $300 a pair and as a serious skater Kristi needed at least two pairs.

But Kristi was finally on the verge of making it beyond the Regional. Already she had advanced to the novice level as a singles skater. Her combination jump was a difficult one for most novices—a triple toe loop and a double toe loop. But Coach Kjarsgaard was conservative. Kristi still had the dreaded compulsories to learn, and she had to mature artistically. Choreographers—people who style dance and free-skating routines—gave her a few lessons about the beat and the rhythm of music. They encouraged her to search for her own music, so that she might interpret them with true feeling. Kristi listened to many different types of instrumental music in order to discover what she liked. According to USFSA rules, amateur skaters could only skate to instrumental music in competition. Vocal music was not allowed, although professional skaters often performed to it during ice shows.

Kristi also had to work on creating themes that matched the music she chose. Every short and long program she skated in competition had to have a theme that she could interpret to the audience with her music, costume, and skating style. Kristi was limited only by her own creativity in coming up with these themes, which could range from ballets like *Swan Lake*, to operas such as *Carmen*, or to more abstract interpretations of a particular dance style, such as flamenco or even bellydancing. One of Kristi's most famous routines was choreographed to the music of *Samson and Delilah*.

Choreographers taught Kristi how to plot her routines on a diagram of the rink so she would use the entire ice surface during her program. Judges often subtracted points from a skater who failed to cover the entire rink while skating. It took Kristi lots of practice to be able to skate confidently near the edge of a rink without accidentally running into the boards or

Kristi was one of only a handful of skaters who performed in both the singles and pairs USFSA competitions. Eventually, trying to succeed at both pairs and singles skating became too much for her.

hitting the rail. As she began to get a feel for the space, and how to skate on it effectively, she was able to skate with speed around the entire rink.

Another aspect of skating control that Kristi mastered was how to land the pairs moves she performed with Rudy. The pairs throws flung her into the air at a greater speed than she gathered when jumping by herself. Learning to land gracefully on one leg after being thrown with not only her own weight, but Rudy's as well, took practice.

Kristi continued to improve as a skater; then in the early months of 1985, her abilities suddenly blossomed. Not yet 14, she won the Central Pacific Regional and Sectional singles, and was on her way to the Nationals. She and Rudy also qualified for the Nationals pairs.

5

TRAGEDIES AND FRUSTRATION

At the 1985 Nationals in Kansas City, Kristi just missed the bronze medal for third place. With Rudy she placed fifth in pairs at the U.S. Junior championship. But her dream of going to the Nationals had been fulfilled. Now she had an even larger dream. At the Nationals everyone talked about how the top three—the medal winners—got to go to the World Championships.

Kristi felt privileged to watch the very best skaters in America. The 1984 Olympian Tiffany Chin won the seniors gold medal that year. Debi Thomas and Caryn Kadavy took silver and bronze. Brian Boitano took the gold in the men's seniors. But the greatest surprise of 1985 came when Kristi and Rudy were invited to the junior Worlds in Sarajevo, Yugoslavia. She and Rudy again placed fifth.

Kristi and her coach Christy Kjarsgaard survey her compulsory figures during a practice session before the 1989 Worlds singles competition in Paris. Kristi placed sixth in the ladies competition.

She and Rudy got even better in 1986, qualifying as juniors for the Nationals on Long Island, New York, where she placed fourth in the singles competition. In the juniors pairs competition, Kristi and Rudy in their red costumes dazzled the judges with side-by-side jumps and spins in which they rotated in opposite directions. The mirror effect was stunning. Kristi and Rudy won the gold medal. Kristi seemed in paradise. At the Worlds for juniors the pair medaled again, this time for third place.

Coach Hulick moved Kristi and Rudy up to seniors in pairs skating. But Coach Kjarsgaard did not want Kristi to move up to seniors in the singles. Her pupil had not yet won a junior medal. That was remedied when Kristi took the silver at the 1987 Nationals in Tacoma, Washington. As seniors in pairs she and Rudy finished fifth. Then in Australia Kristi and Rudy dropped back to the junior level to win the 1987 Worlds, and Kristi won the junior Worlds as a single skater. At 16 she was the best junior skater in the world, but something had been missing from her life. To succeed, Kristi had to put her skating before everything else in her life, including social and school events. She felt isolated from other kids her age and regretted her limited social life. So she went back to school at Mission San Jose High. Still, Kristi's life was never what you could call normal. As Kristi later told *Seventeen* magazine, "I feel like I missed out on the regular high school social life, but that's the way I chose to be." Kristi regretted having to forgo a lot of normal teenage activities, but she was willing to make that sacrifice in order to practice her art and attain her goal of becoming a champion skater.

To make life more complicated for the Yamaguchis, Rudy moved in with them. He was so attached to Kristi, he changed the spelling of his name to Rudi. Kristi and Rudi were like sister and brother.

In 1988 Kristi advanced to the senior level as a single, hoping to qualify for the American Olympic team. But that dream evaporated in Denver, Colorado, when Kristi finished 10th in the singles. Her coach had been right. She wasn't ready for seniors yet. In pairs Kristi and Rudi finished fifth.

Rudi Galindo throws Kristi into the air at the 1989 Worlds in Paris. Kristi competed in the Worlds as both a singles and pairs skater. She placed sixth in singles and fifth in pairs, and was one of only a few skaters to compete in both categories.

Kristi went back to work and won the silver medal in senior singles at the 1989 Nationals in Baltimore. Kristi and Rudi took the gold medal in senior pairs. Kristi was becoming a minor celebrity. ABC-TV had taped a personality profile on her to show with their coverage of the Nationals. *Sports Illustrated* called her "one of the most exciting skating prospects in years." *People Today* dubbed her "a skating sprite with a towering talent" and touted her for the 1992 Olympics. "The Olympics are three years away, and there are always new skaters coming up," she replied, upset by such speculation. She was pleased that Coach Kjarsgaard, her parents, and Rudi were mentioned in the story. Her dad's quote—"Kristi's not much at washing dishes"—amused her.

Kristi's ride up in the skating world took a roller coaster tumble in 1989. She finished sixth at the Worlds in Paris; she and Rudi finished fifth. Then she learned that Coach Kjarsgaard was getting married and moving to Edmonton, Canada. This complication made Kristi's head spin. Jarred by the possible loss of her longtime coach, she reeled when she learned that Coach Hulick had a form of cancer related to AIDS. He was getting thinner every day, and died before the year ended.

Coach Kjarsgaard, now Coach Ness, invited Kristi to come and live with her in Edmonton, where she could train at the Royal Glenora Skating Club. Kristi decided to move to Edmonton. Rudi would fly back and forth to Canada so they could practice their pairs routines. Sometimes Kristi flew to California, too, where the pair trained briefly with John Nicks, a famous coach who had trained pair skating legends Tai Babalonia and Randy Gardner as well as Jo Jo Starbuck and Ken Shelley. Despite their frequent cross-country flights, the distance between Kristi and Rudi was hard to bridge, and their training suffered.

That year Kristi lost George Doi, her maternal grandfather, too. Grandfather Doi had always encouraged her. He was like a rock. Kristi felt like she had been kicked in the teeth.

"[He] used to be the happiest, seeing me go on," Kristi said sadly.

Rudi eventually relocated to Canada so he and Kristi could continue to practice. Their hard work was rewarded in 1990 at the Nationals in Salt Lake City, where Kristi and Rudi won the gold medal again. And Kristi won the silver medal in senior singles, losing again to Jill Trenary.

In the Worlds singles in Nova Scotia she finished fourth, primarily because she placed ninth in the compulsories. But that disappointment was not as bitter as her disappointment in the pairs competition. She and Rudi finished fifth. Kristi felt she was truly stalled. She was not improving in singles or in pairs.

Yet Kristi received an unexpected boost in 1990 when the USFSA announced that compulsory figures would be eliminated from all major skating competitions after July of that year. This was exciting news to Kristi, who had always had trouble with the school figures, which had previously counted for 30% of her score. They were not her favorite part of competition. Indeed, few skaters liked the compulsory figures and many despised them.

In the 1960s, however, compulsory figures were the major factor in scoring skating competitions. Over the years they had decreased in significance, due in large part to the popularity of skating. As more and more people tuned in to televised skating events, they wanted to be daz-

Kristi and Rudi react as their scores are announced and they are declared the gold medal winners at the 1990 Nationals held in Salt Lake City, Utah.

zled by the spins, twirls, and jumps of skaters performing their freestyle programs. No one wanted to watch skaters painstakingly trace school figures on the ice. The tracings were impossible for a television audience to see, anyway. As a result, TV viewers disliked the scoring system for figure skating. When a skater performed brilliantly in the short and long programs but lost to a less dazzling skater who had excelled at compulsories, they did not understand, since the compulsory competitions were rarely televised. Audiences wanted to see the skater who performed best in the freestyle programs to win. The USFSA, which wanted to keep figure skating viewership up, responded to the pressure from audiences and eliminated the compulsory figures.

Now Kristi was able to devote all of her time and energy to perfecting her singles and pairs programs. Even though she felt as though she were getting nowhere, she refused to give up. Kristi Yamaguchi was not a quitter.

6

NEW DIRECTIONS

"You do too much," people in skating had begun to tell her. They said she couldn't succeed at both pairs and singles. Now it seemed as if she had to choose between them.

Her level of success at pairs was about the same as it was for singles. Pairs skating was more dangerous. Several times she had been injured, once knocked unconscious on a triple twist. And she and Rudi had the problem of finding a coach. Besides that, Rudi seemed tormented, not only by Coach Hulick's death but by the possible deaths of his brother, who had AIDS, and of his father, who had heart failure. These torments would have been the very reasons Kristi stuck by him if Rudi had not become so bitter and angry he couldn't practice.

Despite falling on a triple Salchow during her long program at the 1991 Worlds in Munich, Kristi's artistic scores were so high—seven 5.9s and one 6.0—that she won the World Championship.

"Kristi didn't deserve that," Rudi admitted years later about his anger.

Striking out on her own as a singles skater was a major step for Kristi. She wasn't sure she wanted to go in that direction, but she and Rudi had finished in fifth place in pairs for two years in a row and both of them knew how hard it was to break into the top three. Kristi felt that she and Rudi had accomplished as much as they could together. In order to get any better in either singles or pairs, she knew that she would have to choose between them. For years people had been telling her that she tried to do too much. It was a hard decision, but Kristi decided to become a singles skater.

Kristi never stopped having doubts, however. As she told an ABC Sports commentator years later, "To this day I still wonder if it was absolutely the right decision, because I miss pairs terribly. There is something about working with someone out there on the ice and having the same goals together."

Kristi's decision to focus on singles skating brought her to the Nationals in 1991, where she won the short program but was overpowered by Tonya Harding in the long program. Tonya had hit a triple Axel, only the second woman to do it, and the judges were as ecstatic as the crowd.

Kristi was gracious. "I didn't skate that well." she said. But it hit her hard. "A good two weeks after U.S. Nationals, I was a mess on the ice. Almost every day, I had tears. There were comments on my program, maybe it should be changed. I just felt nothing was going to be right, I felt kind of bitter."

There was no time to change her program before the Worlds. Kristi had to bear up under her disappointment and go on to Munich, where she again won the short program. In her long

On the heels of her 1991 World gold win, Kristi captured the gold medal at the Nationals in 1992 and would go on to take the gold at the Olympics.

program she fell on her nemesis, the triple Salchow jump. She felt her program had been perfect except for that. But still the scores startled her. Her technical marks were high in spite of the fall, with five 5.9s. Then the artistic marks hammered her senses: seven 5.9s—and one perfect 6.0.

A shriek pierced the air. "I'm the World Champion."

Her moment of triumph validated all the long hours of practice, all the sacrifices her parents had made for her, and all the loyal support from friends and family. The coming 1992 winter Olympics almost seemed an anti-climax to her. Publicity in national magazines and newspapers no longer excited her. A lot of it was exaggerated, even phony. But the 1991 World Championship was real, and was hers at last.

Early in 1992 Kristi won the 1992 Nationals so convincingly *Sports Illustrated* called it one of the most complete figure skating performances ever seen on American ice. But soon to come was the greatest task of her life: the 1992 winter Olympics. Her World and National championships helped her deal with spells of doubt, especially about her lack of a triple Axel. But Kristi brushed it aside. Her Olympic roommate Nancy Kerrigan helped. The two tried to distract each other from thinking too much about the momentous skating just ahead. Still, occasionally Nancy would yield to a fit of pessimism so ridiculous Kristi just had to laugh. She nicknamed Nancy "Para" for "paranoid," one who is overly suspicious. The two roommates had a great time together.

Kristi usually ran through her entire program twice a day, back-to-back, to build stamina. But after one practice just before the short program of the 1992 Olympics Coach Ness stopped her.

"That's all. You don't have to try to do anything more than what you just did," she said. Her smile seemed two feet wide.

In her short program to "The Blue Danube," wearing her elegant blue and teal costume, Kristi performed all eight required elements to perfection. She launched and landed a combination jump of triple Lutz and double toe loop. She followed with a double flip jump. She

Kristi Yamaguchi took second place at the Lalique Trophy in France in 1991.

reached back on the layback spin and held her skate above her head. She spiraled, then quick-stepped a complex sequence, only to perform a very difficult combination of camel, layback, and sit spin. Finally she landed a double Axel and finished in a spin. Her ears burned from the roar of the crowd. It wasn't just the eight elements but the seamless artistry of the performance that conquered the crowd and the judges. She was a solid first after the short program.

"I'm a little surprised that I'm first," Kristi said. Her roommate Nancy was in second place.

But inside, Kristi was giddy with joy. Years later she admitted she had felt invincible. After her dazzling short program Kristi went on to win the long program with her "wall of 5.9s for artistry." Then she faced her most nervous moments of the entire 1992 Olympics. She realized she didn't have a clue what she was supposed to do during the medal ceremony. She asked Nancy, who had won the bronze, "Do I have to say anything?" Nancy shrugged. Kristi was frozen by doubt. When the ceremony began Nancy had to nudge her forward. But Kristi learned that on the victory podium all she had to do was listen to the strains of the "Star Spangled Banner" as proud Americans in the audience waved their flags.

In the exhibition Kristi dazzled her supporters to "I'm a Yankee Doodle Dandy." The next days were glorious. Her parents gave her a heart shaped ruby and diamond pendant that remains her favorite piece of jewelry. She was interviewed on radio and television. Newspapers and magazines lauded her. One major newspaper wrote that Kristi "interpreted her music, Malagueña, as if the melodies were written on her skates." *Sports Illustrated* echoed the praise, "The judges—and there was no U. S. judge among the nine who arbitrated the women's competition . . . made it clear the direction they wanted to see skating proceed. They loved Yamaguchi's grace and carriage. They loved her speed, her consistency under pressure, the variety of skills displayed during her program. And, yes, they loved her artistry . . . Yamaguchi, without the triple Axel, is as close to a complete package as women's skating ever has seen." *Newsweek* included Nancy Kerrigan in its praise, "Yamaguchi—and Kerrigan nearly so—are simply on a different artistic level, so elegantly dressed, gliding so stylishly, seamlessly, weaving the jumps naturally into their music."

But within two weeks other magazine articles began to question Kristi's American credentials. It began when the agency that tried to get her advertising endorsements complained that she was not getting her share. A business magazine wrote, "Companies may be shying away from Yamaguchi because of her ethnic heritage: she was born in the U. S., as were her folks, but her surname and looks are Japanese." Kristi was stung. She was a fourth-generation American, a California girl. She barely knew where Japan was. She had just competed for America.

Midori Ito of Japan defended Kristi. "Kristi doesn't even speak Japanese, except to say 'good morning.' She's 100 percent American."

Her appearance worked against her in Japan, too. Her mother said that Kristi's agents were turned down by a Japanese car company. They "wouldn't use her because she's Japanese. They wanted that blond-hair, blue-eyed type . . ." Kristi was disturbed by talk about ethnic prejudice. It reminded her of how her father had been forced to live in a camp in a desert along with other Japanese Americans from California for three years during World War II. Her mother had been born in one of the camps.

She was also upset by constant questions about the next Olympics in 1994. Toward the end of 1992 she admitted, "Sometimes, when I was frustrated, I'd think 'Why did I have to win?'" When she decided not to compete in the 1994 Olympics it was not because she had begun to believe she was being discriminated against. Her main reason for not competing was that everyone expected her to win the gold.

Anything less would be considered a failure. That pressure did not appeal to her. And the endorsements had finally started coming. Manufacturers of contact lenses, California raisins, bottled water, sunglasses, cereals, and other food items signed her up to advertise their products.

"I definitely feel that I got my fair share," she said. At 21 Kristi became a professional skater.

Interest in figure skating usually died down right after an Olympics. But in 1994 television executives began promoting skating. Millions of Americans watched the specials.

Kristi joined the most successful professional touring group, "Stars on Ice," run by Scott Hamilton, America's Olympic gold medal winner in 1984. Kristi's other business ventures grew. Besides endorsing products and owning Embarcadero Center Ice Rink on the San Francisco waterfront, she started the Always Dream Foundation that raises money for children. She had homes in Canada and Las Vegas.

On the professional tour many expected the top star to be the 1994 Olympic champion, Oksana Baiul. But she faltered because of injuries. In 1997, Kristi won her fourth World Professional title, skating her winning routine to Elvis Presley's "Trouble." By 1998 Kristi still maintained her supremacy as the most consistently brilliant professional on ice. In "Stars on Ice" she was occasionally paired but her strength was her incomparable single routines. One routine was called "Doop Doop." She skated to techno-pop music, dressed in a black body suit covered by a pink corset vest with tails. Yellow shoulder straps and black and white sleeves made her look wild. Her routine had five triple jumps and six double Axels.

After years of sticking to an exhausting training schedule—which included getting up at

4:00 A.M. to practice before school—Kristi was able to enjoy the comparative freedom that professional skating offered her. With the Stars on Ice tour, Kristi could skate to the music of her choice. For the first time, she could perform routines to popular vocal music, and she did not have to fit required elements into her programs. She was free to be creative. Touring and innovating with other champion skaters was fun for Kristi. Unlike the tense, nervous atmosphere of Olympic competition, professional skating gave Kristi the chance to perform with fewer butterflies in her stomach. She relished the chance to explore her artistic side freely and to perform programs without the stare of the judges upon her. Kristi was one of the most popular skaters on the Stars on Ice tour, and her artistry and dazzling exhibitions delighted audiences.

Words written about her in 1992 were just as true in 1998. Kristi "has mastered nuances of presentation that few other skaters understand: perfect control of her finger tips, the proper tilt of her head—movements that massage the senses."

To put the income from her endorsements and professional career to good use, Kristi started the Always Dream Foundation. With the goal of "inspiring and embracing the dreams of children," the foundation assists organizations that are making a positive difference in children's lives. In recent years, the Always Dream Foundation gave thousands of dollars to groups like SportsBridge, a San Francisco-based non-profit organization that offers after-school programs, summer camps, and mentoring for girls. These programs pair girls up with role models and help them to become better students and athletes. The Always Dream Foundation also

Olympic gold medalists Scott Hamilton and Kristi Yamaguchi pose with friends from the Make A Wish Foundation after skating with the young-sters on ice. Hamilton and Yamaguchi were presented with gold medals handmade by the children.

assists groups devoted to the health and welfare of all disadvantaged and disabled children.

One of the fundraisers Kristi holds each year for her foundation is "Kristi Yamaguchi Skates in the Park," a weekend-long in-line skating festival for families. Held in California, this festival has attracted thousands of children and families to help raise money for a good cause. Kristi also sponsors a "Holiday Wishes Children's Benefit Program" each year at her Embarcadero Center Ice Rink in San Francisco, where children are given Christmas gifts and invited to skate with professional skaters. Proceeds from the Embarcadero Center Ice Rink help to support the Always Dream Foundation.

At 27, Kristi Yamaguchi had become a role model and a professional skater whom many experts regarded as the greatest woman skater in the world.

CHRONOLOGY

1971　Born on July 12 in Hayward, California, with deformed feet.

1976　Ice Show at local mall attracts her to ice skating; Olympic champion Dorothy Hamill becomes her idol.

1977　Places 12th out of 13 in her first competition.

1982　At 11 years old, Kristi adds training for pairs with 13-year-old partner Rudy Galindo and Coach Jim Hulick.

1985　Begins private tutoring at home. Places fourth at Nationals in novice singles, fifth in junior pairs.

1987　Wins National junior singles, World junior pairs. Returns to high school at Mission San Jose.

1989　At Nationals Kristi wins silver in singles, gold in pairs. Graduates high school, follows singles coach to Canada.

1991　Wins World singles championship.

1992　Wins gold at Winter Olympics.

1993　Turns professional.

1994　World Pro Figure Skating Champion.

1996　World Pro Figure Skating Champion; Establishes the "Always Dream" Foundation, an organization whose mission is to encourage and support the hopes and dreams of children.

1997　World Pro Figure Skating Champion.

1998　Inducted into the US Figure Skating Hall of Fame

1999　Wins the Make a Wish Grantor Recognition for the Year Award.

2000　Marries Florida Panther Bret Hedican.

2002　Serves as Goodwill Ambassador for the Winter Olympics in Salt Lake City, Utah.

FURTHER READING

Brennan, Christine. *Inside Edge*. New York: Scribner, 1996.

Coffey, Frank and Filip Bondy. *Dreams of Gold: The Nancy Kerrigan Story*. New York: St. Martin's, 1994.

Donohue, Shiobhan. *Kristi Yamaguchi*. Minneapolis: Lerner Publications Company, 1994.

Gutman, Dan. *Ice Skating: From Axels to Zambonis*. New York: Viking, 1995.

Hagan, Patricia, editor. *Spalding Figure Skating: Sharpen Your Skills*. Indianapolis: Masters Press, 1995.

Harris, Ricky. *Choreography and Style for Ice Skaters*. New York: St. Martin's Press, 1980.

Ogilvie, Robert. *Basic Ice Skating Skills: An Official Handbook Prepared for the United States Figure Skating Association*. Philadelphia: J. B. Lippincott, 1968.

Petkevich, John Misha. *Sports Illustrated Figure Skating: Championship Techniques*. New York: Winner's Circle Books, 1989.

Yamaguchi, Kristi, with Christy Ness and Jody Meacham. *Figure Skating for Dummies*. Foster City, California: IDG Books Worldwide, Inc., 1997.

ABOUT THE AUTHOR

Sam Wellman lives in Kansas. He has degrees from colleges in the Midwest and the Ivy League. He has written a number of biographies of notable people, as diverse as George Washington Carver, Mother Teresa, Christopher Columbus, and Michelle Kwan—for both adults and younger readers.

GLOSSARY

AXEL: a jump named for its inventor, Axel Paulsen. The Axel is the only jump launched while skating forward. A skater takes off from the forward outside skate edge and lands on the opposite foot on a back outside edge. A double Axel is the same jump with two and a half mid-air rotations. A triple Axel, achieved for the first time in 1978, requires three and a half mid-air rotations.

CAMEL: a skating spin performed with one leg extended back; the camel is called a flying camel when a skater jumps into the spin.

CROSSOVER: performed when a skater crosses his or her stride; a crossover tends to increase a skater's speed.

DEATH SPIRAL: a pairs figure skating move in which the man pivots and spins the woman in a circle around him with one hand while her arched body spirals down until it is almost parallel to the ice.

FLIP: a jump made by sticking the blade pick into the ice, revolving, and then landing on the back outside edge of the toe-assisting foot; the triple flip is the same jump with three revolutions.

FOOTWORK: any series of turns, steps, hops, and crossovers done at high speed.

LIFTS: pairs moves in which the man holds the woman up in a ballet-like position over his head; variations on lifts include the star lift, in which the woman holds both her arms in the air, and the one-armed lift, in which the man supports the woman with only one arm.

LOOP: a jump in which the skater takes off and lands on the same back outside edge.

LUTZ: a jump named for its creator, Alois Lutz. For the Lutz, a skater takes off on a back outside edge, revolves, and then lands on a back outside edge. When a skater revolves three times in the air, the jump is called a triple Lutz.

SALCHOW: a jump named after Swedish skater Ulrich Salchow. For the Salchow, a skater makes a long glide backward and then takes off on the outside edge of one skate, with a boost from the toe of the opposite skate. After revolving, the skater lands on the outside edge of the boosting skate. A double Salchow has two rotations; a triple Salchow requires three full rotations while in the air.

SPIN: a skater performs a spin by rotating from one fixed point; when skaters spin, they move so fast their image becomes blurred.

SIT SPIN: a spin in which the skater crouches down, balanced on one leg while the other extends; often a skater will pull up out of a sit spin to a standing spin position.

SPREAD-EAGLE: a move in which a skater glides on two feet, with the lead foot on a forward edge and the trail foot on the same edge, only backward.

TOE LOOP: a jump launched off the toe pick of the free foot in which a skater completes one rotation and lands on the back outside edge of the same foot. The toe pick can launch the skater to a great height; hence, a double toe loop has two mid-air rotations, and a triple toe loop has three.

THROWS: pairs moves in which the man throws the woman into the air, where she spins two or three times before landing on one foot.

INDEX